FINGERPICKING *Mozart*

ISBN 978-1-4234-1045-4

Visit Hal Leonard Online at www.halleonard.com

In Australia Contact:
Hal Leonard Australia Pty. Ltd.
4 Lentara Court
Cheltenham, Victoria, 3192 Australia
Email: ausadmin@halleonard.com

HAL•LEONARD®
CORPORATION
7777 W. BLUEMOUND RD. P.O. BOX 13819 MILWAUKEE, WI 53213

Air in A-Flat Major

K109b, No. 8
from THE LONDON NOTEBOOK
By Wolfgang Amadeus Mozart

*Capo I
Moderately

*This arrangement in G major for playability. To play in A♭ major, capo 1st fret.

Laudate Dominum

from VESPERAE SOLENNES

By Wolfgang Amadeus Mozart

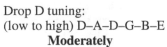

Drop D tuning:
(low to high) D–A–D–G–B–E

Moderately

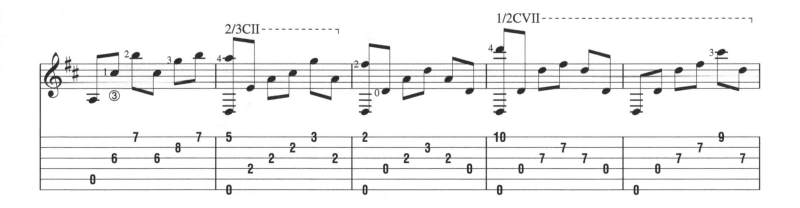

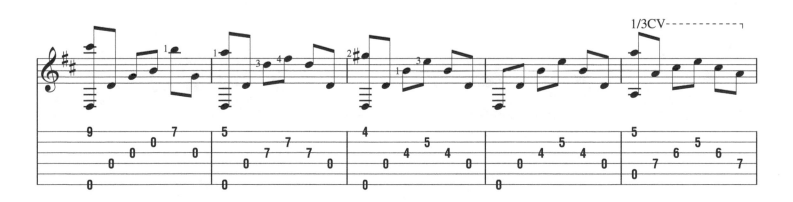

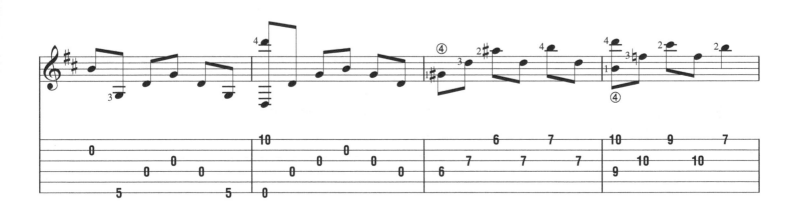

Ave verum

(Jesu, Word of God Incarnate)

By Wolfgang Amadeus Mozart

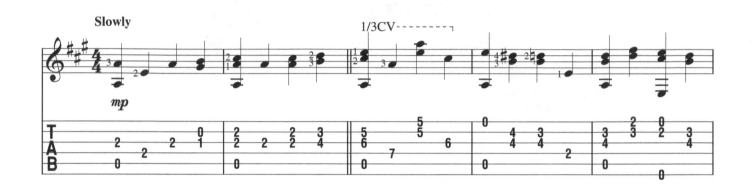

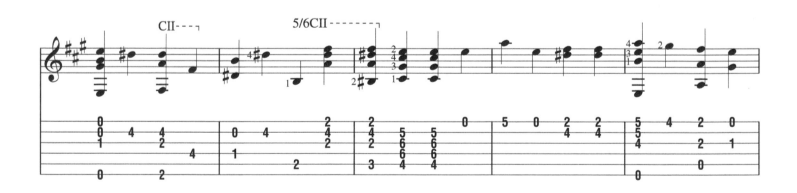

Deh vieni alla finestra
(Serenade)
from DON GIOVANNI

By Wolfgang Amadeus Mozart

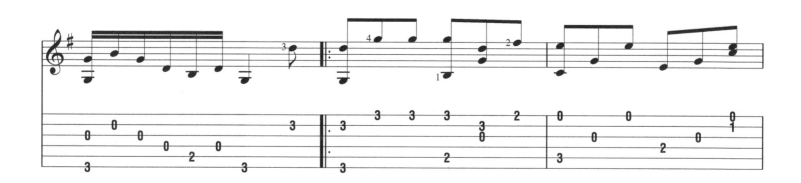

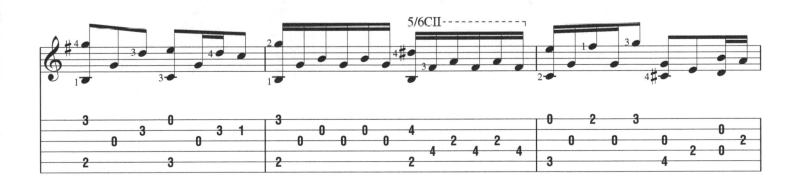

Eine kleine Nachtmusik

By Wolfgang Amadeus Mozart

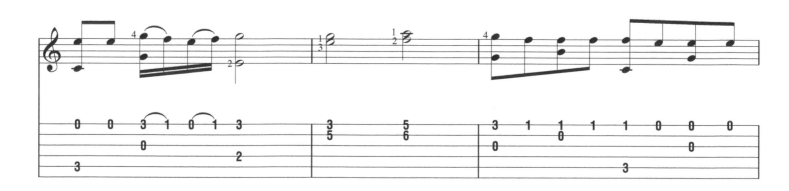

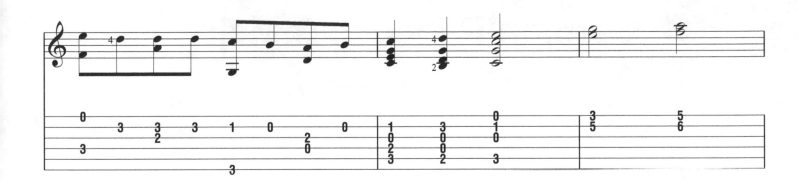

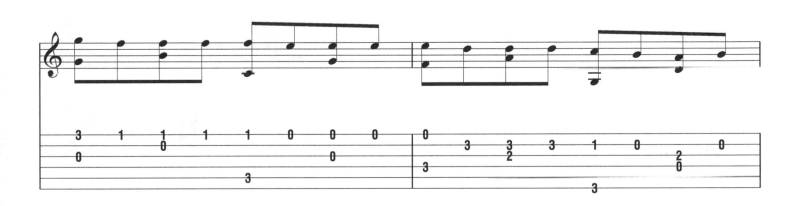

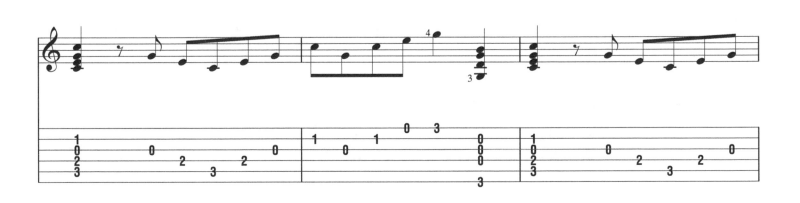

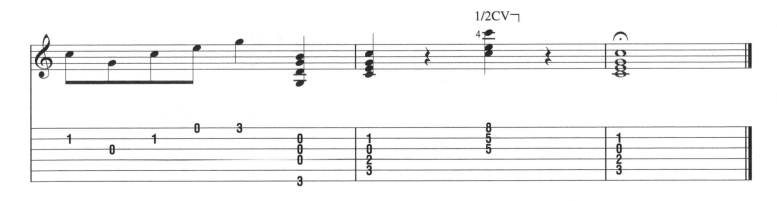

German Dance in C Major

K605, No. 3

By Wolfgang Amadeus Mozart

*This arrangement in G major for playability. To play in C major, capo 5th fret.

2nd time, D.C. al Fine

Minuet in F Major
K. 2
By Wolfgang Amadeus Mozart

*Capo VIII
Moderately

*This arrangement in A major for playability. To play in F major, capo 8th fret.

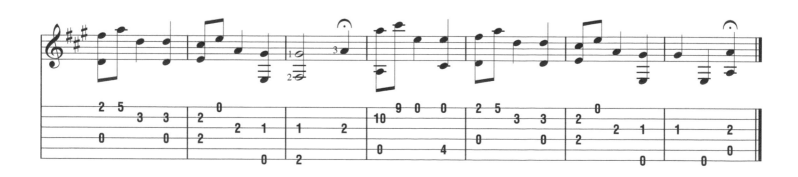

Piano Concerto No. 21 in C Major ("Elvira Madigan"), Second Movement Excerpt

By Wolfgang Amadeus Mozart

Drop D tuning, *down 1 step:
(low to high) D–A–D–G–B–E

Slowly

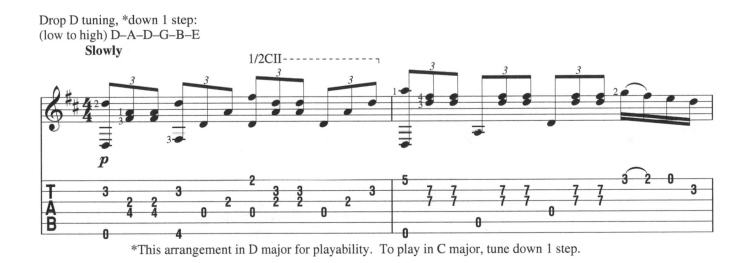

*This arrangement in D major for playability. To play in C major, tune down 1 step.

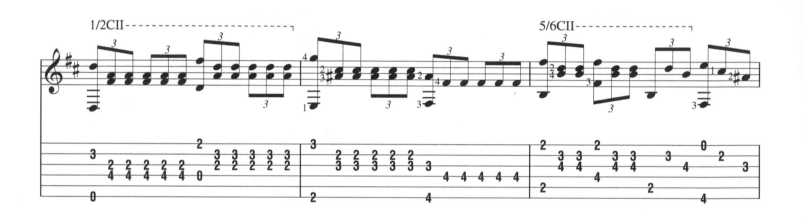

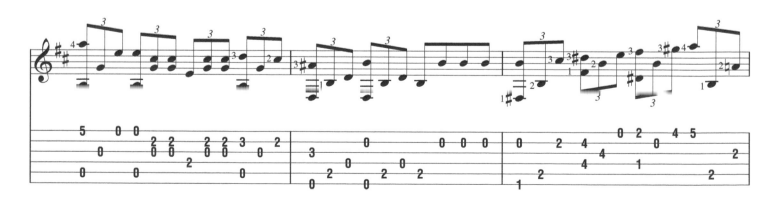

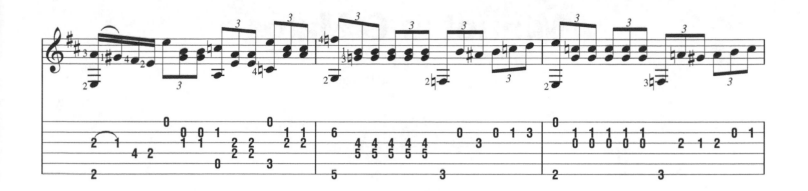

2/3CI - - - - - - - - - - -

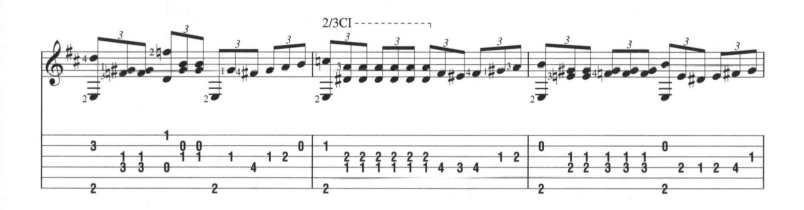

1/2CII - - - - - - - - - - -

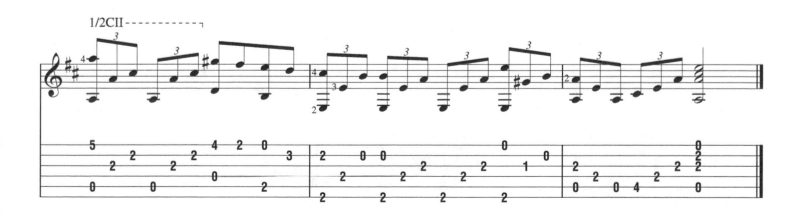

Minuet in G Major

K. 1

By Wolfgang Amadeus Mozart

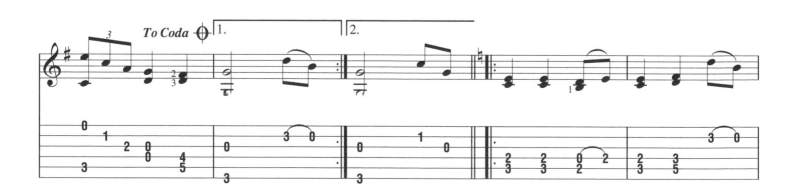

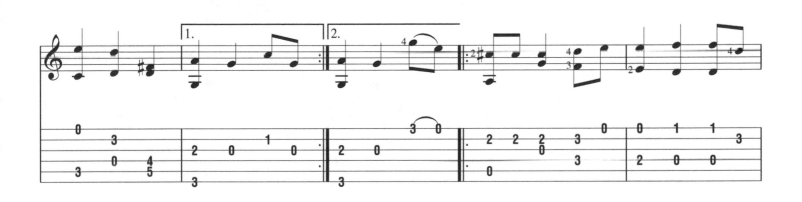

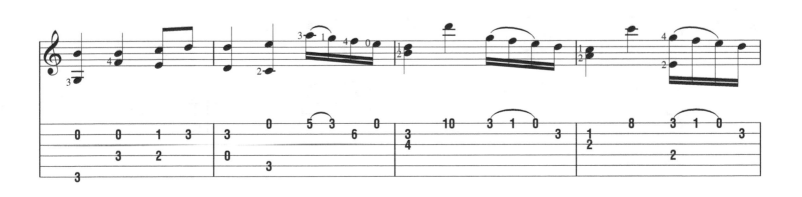

Papageno's Song

from THE MAGIC FLUTE (DIE ZAUBERFLOTE)

By Wolfgang Amadeus Mozart

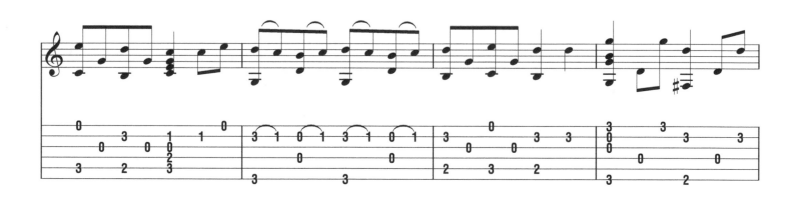

Piano Sonata in A

By Wolfgang Amadeus Mozart

*Capo II

Moderately

*This arrangement in G major for playability. To play in A major, capo 2nd fret.

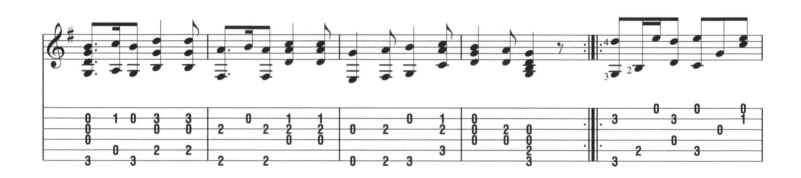

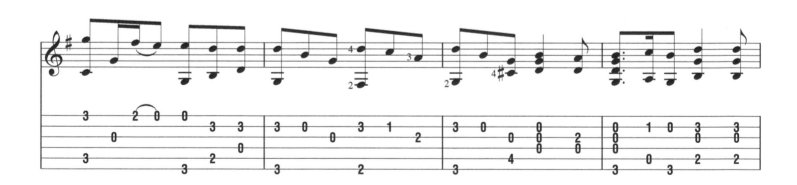

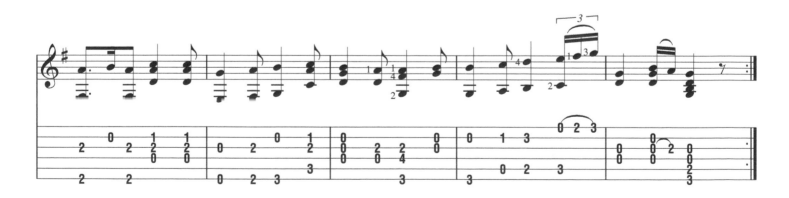

Piano Sonata in C

By Wolfgang Amadeus Mozart

*Capo V

Slowly

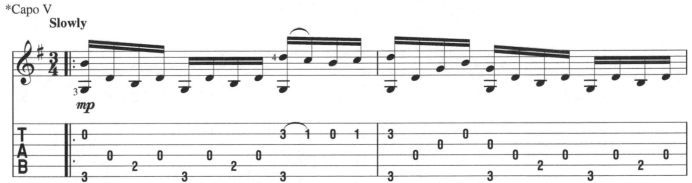

*This arrangement in G major for playability. To play in C major, capo 5th fret.

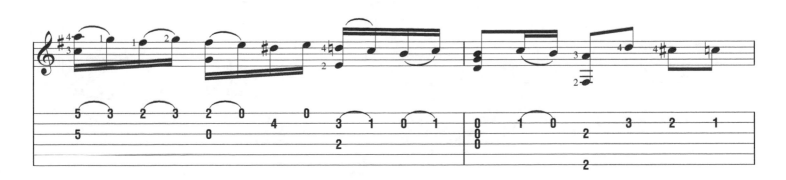

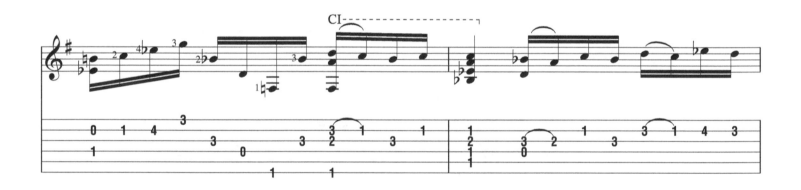

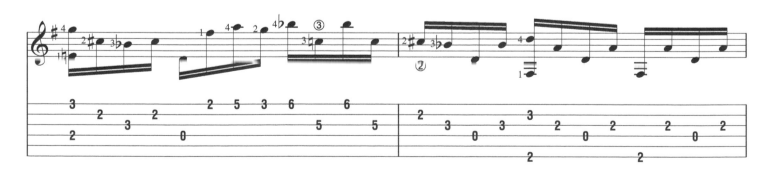

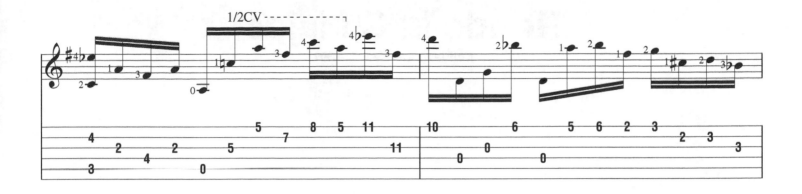

D.C. al Coda

⊕ Coda

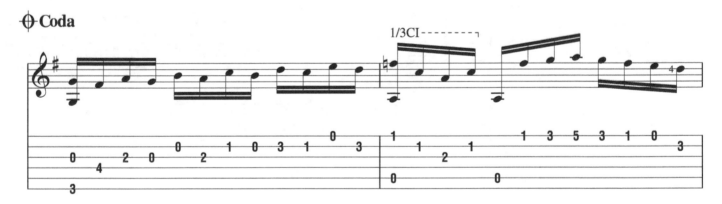

Rondo in C Major

By Wolfgang Amadeus Mozart

*Capo III

Moderately

*This arrangement in A major for playability. To play in C major, capo 3rd fret.

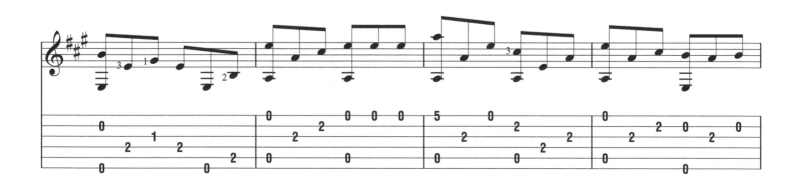

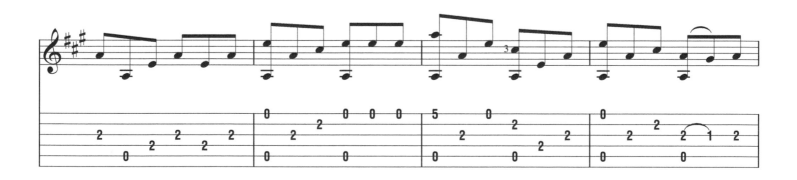

Voi, che sapete

from LE NOZZE DI FIGARO (THE MARRIAGE OF FIGARO)

By Wolfgang Amadeus Mozart

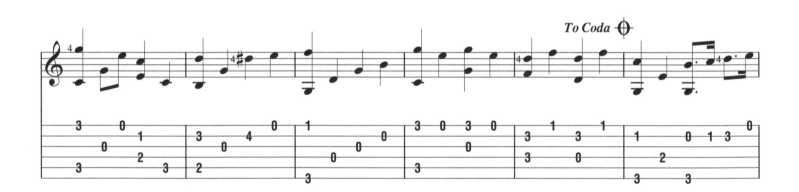

D.C. al Coda

Coda

Second Movement Theme
from Clarinet Concerto
By Wolfgang Amadeus Mozart

Drop D tuning:
(low to high) D–A–D–G–B–E

Slowly

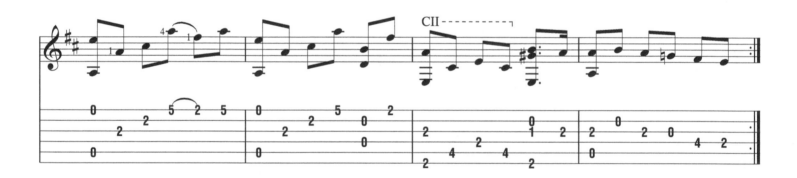